Disney
Beauty AND the Beast

MUSIC FROM THE MOTION PICTURE SOUNDTRACK

Music by ALAN MENKEN
Lyrics by HOWARD ASHMAN and

T0079366

ISBN 978-1-5400-0072-9

Motion Picture Artwork, TM & Copyright
© 2017 Disney

Wonderland Music Company, Inc.
Walt Disney Music Company

DISTRIBUTED BY

HAL•LEONARD®

7777 W. BLUEMOUND RD. P.O. BOX 13819 MILWAUKEE, WI 53213

In Australia Contact:
Hal Leonard Australia Pty. Ltd.
4 Lentara Court
Cheltenham, Victoria, 3192 Australia
Email: ausadmin@halleonard.com.au

Visit Hal Leonard Online at
www.halleonard.com

OVERTURE

Music by ALAN MENKEN

4

(𝅗𝅥 = 𝅘𝅥)

Moderately, expressively

p

(R.H. over L.H.)

rit.

rall.

mp a tempo

MAIN TITLE: PROLOGUE
(Pt. 1 and Pt. 2)

Music by ALAN MENKEN

Moderately
PROLOGUE PT. 1

PROLOGUE PT. 2
Music by ALAN MENKEN
and CHRISTOPHER BENSTEAD

ARIA

Music by ALAN MENKEN
Lyrics by TIM RICE

BELLE

Music by ALAN MENKEN
Lyrics by HOWARD ASHMAN

GASTON

Music by ALAN MENKEN
Lyrics by HOWARD ASHMAN

Freely

Barroom Waltz, in 1

BE OUR GUEST

Music by ALAN MENKEN
Lyrics by HOWARD ASHMAN

Slower, melancholy

mp freely

DAYS IN THE SUN

Music by ALAN MENKEN
Lyrics by TIM RICE

SOMETHING THERE

Music by ALAN MENKEN
Lyrics by HOWARD ASHMAN

BEAUTY AND THE BEAST

Music by ALAN MENKEN
Lyrics by HOWARD ASHMAN

THE MOB SONG

Music by ALAN MENKEN
Lyrics by HOWARD ASHMAN

HOW DOES A MOMENT LAST FOREVER

(As performed by Celine Dion)

Music by ALAN MENKEN
Lyrics by TIM RICE

EVERMORE
(As performed by Josh Groban)

Music by ALAN MENKEN
Lyrics by TIM RICE